# A BROKEN-HEARTED SCHIZOPHRENIC

## CATHERINE E. GOIN

WESTBOW
PRESS°
A DIVISION OF THOMAS NELSON
& ZONDERVAN

WestBow Press books may be ordered through booksellers or by contacting:

WestBow Press
A Division of Thomas Nelson & Zondervan
1663 Liberty Drive
Bloomington, IN 47403
www.westbowpress.com
844-714-3454

Cover art: Catherine E. Goin

ISBN: 978-1-6642-5856-3 (sc)
ISBN: 978-1-6642-5855-6 (e)

Library of Congress Control Number: 2022903380

Print information available on the last page.

WestBow Press rev. date: 03/11/2022

*Lass, if to sleep you would repair*
*As peaceful as you woke,*
*Best not besiege your lover there*
*For just the words he spoke*
*To me, that's grown so free from care*
*Since my heart broke!*

*From 'The Merry Maid' by Edna St. Vincent Millay*

*Dedicated to my wonderful doctors:*
*Dr. Schwartz, Dr. Stanley Wang, Dr. Zigmund Lebensohn,*
*and Dr. David Goldstein.*

# CONTENTS

# FOREWORD

Writing poetry is immensley important in my life. It gives clarity to my scary shizophbrenic brain, and helps me express insights, plans and designs that are improtant to me and my ability to experience happiness.

I decided to put these poems into order so that I could tell others how I experienced the descent into madness and the help I received in overcoming it to live an orderly somewhat normal life.

The poems in this little book are the tip of the iceberg. After putting them in order, I got the brilliant idea to do a memoir (not just of events, but of thoughts) of my life which is drawing to a close. I hope you, my reader, enjoy reading them as much as I enjoyed writing them.

# AT NIGHT ON THE PLANE

After properly introducing themselves, we three young stewardesses
sat in the front lounge of the DC-10 at the lounge table, and whiled
away the time playing cards, eating caviar and singing;

Oh, mighty sturgeon from the Caspian Sea
We love thy roe, thy eggs love we.

Sitting so black on the crispy bread
While sipping champagne it goes to our heads.

Some prefer vodka, we do not really care,
Both make us happy, we do declare,

For purists like we, the roe alone is fine.
We arrange it on toast, in a straight little line.

Others like egg yolk and white crumbled in bits
And a touch of onion as it passes the lips.

Oh caviar, caviar, food of the gods
We are happy to eat it, though we are but clods.

Some think it too salty, but certainly not we
We love you, oh sturgeon, from the Caspian Sea.

We love you,
We love you,
Do we!

# MADAME PELE AND WAHU

Madame Pele was somewhat perplexed
As her muscles she flexed
She was eager to take a walk
On this rock in the middle of the Pacific...
The terrific Pacific.
Pele with her flaming tresses,
Pele with her blazing dresses.
Pele looked down—flame.
To waste precious fire is a shame.

Wahu he prances, perchances
He will see me!
Sitting quietly by the sea.
At night, only lava light!
While the water laps along the shore
While the waves in the distance roar.
The ships go out to sea...
The ships go out to see....

Still the molten lava grumbles
Still the molten lava mumbles
As down the moimtainside it stumbles
It oozes—tearing down the trees
It oozes—bringing kahunas to their knees.

They know their gods
Are constructs of myth and lore
Created in the days of yore!

While the lava, flowing lava

Spreading o'er the Earth
While the Sea gives birth
To the motintains and the islands
In the middle of the ocean...
Swaying, swaying motion.

Wahu continued on his jaunts
Across the moimtain tops—his haunts.
He carried a bone between his teeth
He had found it underneath
The log that sat upon the mountaintop...
Sitting there...
Not a care....

He carried the bone between his teeth.
He had found it underneath
The log that sat upon the mountaintop....
      Sitting there....
      Not a care...
      Sitting there.

Wahu is white with circles of black
Around his eyes and on his back
The pads of his feet are pink
As into the lava they sink.

I sat! Waves lapping on the shore.
Was there more of Pele and Wahu
Drifting through my mind?
I was blind with fear
      Of delusions so near.
      Of illusions so near.

The lava, up into the air it shot!
It was hot!
It tore off the mountain top.
Throughout the volcanic evening,
Among the rocks and trees they went weaving.
Pele and Wahu continued to walk.
He would bark and she would talk…

"Goodness, gracious," I said, sitting straight up in bed, sweat pouring down my face and back, my heart beating frantically. "What was that?" I screamed.

Muffy Kay, my cousin was yelling at me, "Wake up, ! You were dreaming! It is a good thing that I am here. Your mother tells me that you have fallen off the deep end. So, I am just the right person to be with you right now."

"Oh, Muffy Kay! I am so glad that you are here. Now I do not need to be afraid."

# My Troubles Just Begun

OH!! Holy Father???? 3 in 1????
I rue the day my troubles begun.
They came—"surprise!"
Tumbling and stumbling before my eyes....

Voices! Voices!
Think! Think!
Where, oh where could they be hid?
Oh! Of them to be rid.

Down, down it fell;
Thistleweed survived the tumult of the seed.

Leaves float down like gossamer dust,
Terra, Terra, shades to the sound of rust...
.. .rust...loud and clear
Settled on the dirt so near------me, help me
Help me dear so nearly, meer—
-ly the souind of thunder, tearing the land asunder.

Asunder, yes! Asunder, why?
Asunder sing out, laugh and cry! Until I die.

Die! Why?
You reply

"Because I say so! That is why."

# JUMP!

I looked down
    down
        down
The bridge is very high
I know I can fly!
The bridge is very high!

The last time
    I tried to fly
I fell onto some rocks.
My body was seriously convulsed
    by shuddering shocks.

It turned out
    I broke a rib or two
I really, really tried to fly
What is a girl to do?

The voices were persistent
The voices were consistent.

Jump!
    Jump!
        Jump!

Get out of your slump!

Shall I ?
    Shall I ?
        Shall I ?

Jump?

# DARK NIGHT OF THE SOUL

The coffee had finally finished brewing, and the lovely aroma of Viennese Cinnamon drifted throughout the apartment. I had developed a taste for more exotic blends, no longer just the black swill that Dad and I used to drink in the early mornings when we sat and talked before the sun rose, and he went to work

"I have not thought about him for the longest time. I wonder if I am oppressed."

I was hmgry and was reaching for an apple when a Voice thundered throughout my mind,

"You are not normal!"

The world crashed around me—

"I am not normal. What shall I do?

What is wrong? What is wrong? I am so confused."

I lit a cigarette, and watched the smoke rings drift from my mouth into the air.

Voices whispered in my ears, strange voices I did not understand.

"It is

Easter and I should be going to church, but right now I am angry at how I have treated

God, and I feel in total disgrace, so I would not be welcome at church....

I cannot bear feeling this way...

I shall not stay this way...

I blew another smoke ring and coughed...a song appeared in my heart....

I hope when I die
God will take me to the sky.
I can drift from cloud to cloud

Never being very loud.
I can drift from cosmos to cosmos
Searching for the origen of fleas
How they brought the dog and cat world
To its knees.
And travel through time
At the drop of a hat.
I love to google, I do love that.

My heart lifted for a moment by the beautiful song which I had
heard in my heart.
Then sadness....
There has been too much death
In your yoimg life.
You are bereft by death.

Then the fog lifted and the blue sky was peeping out from the
gloom. For a moment my spirit was cheered...

It did not feel oppressed
Inappropriately dressed
Totally psychologically messed.

Then darkness. I sat on the floor, sqxiatting on my heels as I had
learned to do in Yoga class...
Rocking back and forth, chanting...

I have betrayed you, God!
    Strike me dead.
I have lived too long,
    Wrong,
    Strike me dead!
I have lost my song.
    Strike me dead.

I continued to rock back and forth. I knew that God had heard me. I knew my days were nimibered....

But!

The Voices stopped!

# A Fight, One Night

Upon one dark, mysterious night
Two young gents
      with knives did fight.
The knives did flick!
The knives did flash!
As through the air
      their knives did slash.

The maiden fair
She did declare
"These guys are surely nuts.
I, for one, am splitting the scene!
No 'ifs', no 'ands', no 'huts'."

Long did they fight on that glorious night.
The maiden fair had split.
Still, on they fought
Although they knew they ought to quit.

The knives did flick, the knives did flash!
A rip appeared upon a shirt.
One of the combatants had been hurt!

He jumped and howled and screamed
      With pain!
Suddenly the crowd yelled "rain!"

The crowd, you see,
Was much like me—
      In that—

A fight brought out their worst!
It seems a condition
Of the human situation
To be thus—ally accursed.

I cannot 'git'
          Over him,
Even though I know
          I am slim!

What came over me?
That I should flip
Head over heels for Lee?

He certainly was a handsome dude
Who hated me!
How rude!
How crude!

I have given it a lot of thought
How I was lucky not to have been shot!
And left to rot
          On the pier by the Bay

But...'
He considered me to be mad
Baying and chirping at the moon....
          Croon, croon, croon...

Here I sit, many moons later
Still not over that woman-hater!
Though to give the Lee his due
It is true that
          He was not dull!

Not at all!
That is probatly why I did fall
Head over heels for him
Back then, when I was slim.

Momma Mia
I am still not recovered from Lee-ah,
Or him from me-ah.

If he is still walking on the face of the Earth,
Please, Dear God, give me wide berth.
As I hope to live a year or two more,
So that I can even the score.

I can not forget him,
Even though I am now slim.
He bored into my heart...
He riveted my soul
  With his stories of the glories
  Of the world on film...
   Click....
   Click....
   Click...

Did he not xmderstand that I was Sick?
And terrified that I had died,
  And gone to be fried?
He pushed me,
And I landed on the floor
And hit my head
  Am I or am I not dead?
  Am I or am I not dead?

Lights went off and drifted around

Inside my crown...
Lights flickering, red and blue
And every other hue.

Therefore...
Momma Mia!
help me to get over Lee-ah!.

# THE APARTMENT

It was a groovy apartment, and had a fire escape out of a second
story window.
By now I was beginning to exhibit the urmiistakable signs of
schizophrenia, the paranoid variety...

Voices loud, voices clear
Voices there and voices here
Voices everywhere
I do declare.

The apartment was a gleamy apparition
  Showing no contrition
  Showing no ambition
  Showing no ammunition.

The telephone would ring
And I would cry
I really would have loved to die
I had not reached the understanding of "why."

The apartment was quiet inside
  And noisy on the street.
The neighborhood danced to a
  Daffodil beat
For only six hours each day did I have heat.

It was well decorated
Perfect for a nervous breakdown.
It was fated....
        And
              Then
                      There
                            Was
                                  Lee,
                                        He

Caused me to distract
He moved in
There was no turning back

Alcohol dulled his voice.
It fried his brain

It ruined his mind
It absolutely,
        Positively
                Was not kind.

"Help! Help!
        I need help.
My brain is tingling
        Under my scalp!"

Reverberated through my mind...
These thoughts were not kind.

The thoughts crept into
        Each little cell
I knew these little thoughts
        So well.

"I wish. Dear Lee,
  That you would leave
And I could have some time
  To grieve
About the deaths of dogs and cats,
And even about the deaths of bats."

These fearsome thoughts
Which made life alarming
Swiftly through my soul
  Were swarming.
I did not find them charming.

I knew that Lee would have to go.
Quickly,not so fearsome slow.
I had a hunch that he would punch
  And kick
      And scream
          And shout
I had to throw him out.
It broke my heart, indeed it did
I fancied myself
  In love with the kid.

In February I finished the chore
And successftilly kicked him
Out the door.

Quiet flowed into the apartment. It did not give a hint
Of all the ideas,
  Both right and wrong
That would pound in the brain

Each night—
    For so long
Each would have a song.

"Help! Help!
I need help!
My brain is tingling
Under my scalp!"

The phone rang each day at four.
Voices would hiss and squack
They did not always talk....
        At least not much.

A loner, a loner—now a loner.
The time had come to evaporate
        No longer to contemplate
        No longer to congregate
        No longer to placate.

The time had come to meditate....
        To jump
A persistent theme
It appeared in each and every dream.
Night and day
The voices would not go away.

"Help! Help!
I need help!
My brain is tingling under my scalp!"

# My Heart is Made of Icy Rock

If it should melt
I'd go into shock
It would shatter, go into free-fall
Nothing left of me at all.
????shatter,
      Free fall...
             Nothing left of me at all??!

@@@
my mom says I overreact
      And
Should cut myself some slack.

i protest, "Why, you know i'm cool. Yes, you know%%%%
Still, into my heart your opinion flows.
$$$$
"Misery loves company, "i've always heard
Yes indeedy, my parameters are blurred.

Blurred—the edges
      Shimmering
      Glimmering
While the gossamer dust dances
On the window pane prances...

I look on—filled with awe
Wondering, "Is it really dust I saw?
      Or is it more?
      Of an ethereal bent?
A sign —to me

A sign—a portent
Which lately to me has been sent
Dancing gently in the air
Using too much of the oxygen
We both share????
Of the air....

Oh, Gossamer Dust
    Please do nqt rust

# THE 16TH FLOOR

I will think about Star Trek and Mr. Spock. His ears are a lot like mine....He is a space alien and thusly seems real to me... .1 was in contact with some of them until I came to the hospital... .Star Trek is such a wonderful show... .All of the people on the 16th Floor with me love it (even Miss Princess Olga from St. Petersburg).. ..I wonder if the nurses and doctors identify with Bones... He is humorous... .Captain Kirk is swashbuckling....But my favorite is Spock....a master of logic....! need logic....

> From my position in the hears and nows
> I must get rid of my sacred cows.
> Logic is to be desired
> Logic is to be admired
> My mind is much mired
> I am lucky I was not fired
> If they knew then
> What they know now
> I would not have been hired.

Oh, to be logical! How does one get that way? Well, perhaps by focusing. Now that is an interesting concept....focusing... to focus...
>    To focus on jumping
>    To focus on flying

Are they related? It would seem that after jumping, for a short time one might think that one is flying—whereas in actuality one would be falling! This is so confusing.

One forgets about the end result of jumping—if the distance is great enough... .splat!

My thoughts about life before.....falling.. .asleep....

How did I get here? I do not know.
Was there an ambulance? Was it slow?

Did the sirens scream and wail
As they transported me from the jail?

For a fact my life was a mess
God saw a real live damsel in distress.

He got me to the 16th Floor
He got me a Chinese Baptist doctor
He need not do more.
Dr. Sung was small and sleek
He moved around the floor so quick
He gave me a shot and said
"You should be grateful
You are not dead. But, cheer up.
Things will get better I always say
When the sun shines down
On a brand new day.

After a day or two you will not scream
All of this will seem like a dream...
A confusing one if I do say so
Rehabilitation will be slow.
Do not get discouraged
Do not get depressed
Put on fashionable clothes
When you get dressed.
Eat your meals, smoke if you must
When you get better you will
Stop smoking, I trust.

Go to sleep and enjoy a good dream
For goodness sake, please do not scream.

The other patients need their rest
Try really hard not to be a pest.

I tossed and turned in my bed. The stars swept across the night sky. Looking out of the window, I could see the North Star in the cold, dark night, "I think I will eat some pancakes with blueberries in the morning for breakfast....

I wish I had a cat... .1 wish my roommate Lucy would not cry... .as Kristen McMenaney said, "Je suis rousse, et alors?" or, "I am a redhead! So!"

# RESPECTABILITY

I trailed alongside Dr. Sung as we walked down the corridor to the lounge where everyone was gathered to watch Star Trek—The Trouble with Tribbles. "You need to watch this show as it points out the importance of moderation, which is a good philosophy for you. It does wonders for the digestion." Clearly I thought, Dr. Sung has the Asian attitude—a little bit of Zen and a little bit of Zat.

Dr. Sung was happy with his little success. This was the only way to get me to participate with the group.

An hour later I was back in my room. The light was out when into my head popped a philosophical poem about respectability.

> Traveling through the sky,
> Oh, how I love to fly
> When the sky is black
> It is night and the coffee cup is hot
> In it there is a shot.. .of espresso
>
> This atmosphere will be the death of me
> Radioactivity is free. It is in the air
> It is everywhere.
>
> The coffee they serve bolsters up my nerve
> Have you thought, ever,
> About the weather?
> And how cold the air is outside
> As you take this mysterious
> Magic carpet ride?

Through the air
At night, not light

An hour later the poem was finished
I was proud of accomplishing something
I was tired
I retired
For the night
Tomorrow I will get up and continue the fight.

Click, click
Out went the light.

# PLACE

It came as quite a shock to me
To be inside this place
Because to 'polite society'
'mental' is a disgrace.

'mental'—yes. It is a state
Of confusion and undo stress
To be quite truthful. Myself was a mess.
A mess
Yes, a mess
I must confess

The walls were white
The doors were bolted
So we could not escape
So we would be halted

There were no pictures on the walls
They were so very bare
It was hard for me to credit
That I was really there.
That I was really there.

One day 'doc' came.
There had been rain.
The day was dark and gloomy.
The bed and room in which
I lay my head was spare and not so roomy.
But it was all I had.
I was too sick to be sad.

'doc' looked at me and said,
"I think you need to get out more.
It is not helpful to stare at the door.
It is not helpful to glare at the door.
So follow me and we will see "Star Trek"
With all the others
Whom you should meet!
Whom you should greet!

They all have a story—a history—
Why they ended up here is still a mystery."

# GRACE

"Oh my" I cry
Looking skyward from my bed
"Why am I not dead?
The sky looks odd as seen
From behind bars
It looks black-striped and tired."

"Oh my," I cry
Looking upwards from my bed
"Why did I not die?
Tell me why!'"

Doc's next job was really hard—
To make me gain some weight—
So this is what he said,
"You can eat or you are dead!"

I don't know why
I had no reply.
God's grace descended upon
Me before I was gone.

So! I ate!

# SPACE

He wrapped his air around him
He slid off into space.
I never really saw him,
I only saw his face.

I never really knew him
I will tell you why
He was just my doctor
He taught me not to cry...
unless the circumstances
Warranted it

He wrapped his aura on his head
Always did he wear it
Even into bed.
He absolutely would not share it.
He was a most miraculous 'doc'
He even got me out of shock.

# MODD SAYS

**A voice appeared in my head**
**And said;**
**My name is Modd.**
"I must say
      her life appears a mess-
A real live maiden
      in distress.
Unless I choose
      to get involved
It is unlikely
      her problem will be solved

I will jump right in,
      help her out.
That is what Modd's life
      is all about

                I said;

"The doctor said
I must be fed
Unless instead
I wish to be dead.

I thought about this.
It is quite a twist.
He says I must work hard
To gain some lard.

I do not want to jump
And land with
        a thump
                and a bump,
I wish indeed
        to live awhile
And most important,
        do it in style"

                Modd Says

"Right on kid.
I dig
Your spirit,
Oh, so big.

Eat with my blessing.
It takes out the guessing
On how to gain weight.
To be thin is not your fate."

                I said;

"Gracious me!
I do declare!
I have nothing to wear!
My hospital wardrobe
        is quite small
I hardly have
        anything at all
In my size.

I Continued;

Oh, Modd most wise
You know that
        talking with Modd
Seems a little odd."

Modd Then Says

"Talking with you
Seems peculiar too."

# NO IFS, ANDS, OR BUTS.

The doctor agreed and your mother concurred
That to eat is to live
Good health it can give.
To the alternative it is preferred.

It makes your nails longer
It makes your hair stronger.
We all realize the society
Does not help
A young lady
Take good care of herself.

Besides it is fun to fill yourself up.
Just do not eat more than your stomach can store.
Because that leads to fat, and we all know
That that is to be avoided
No matter the reason
No matter the season
Fat in the airlines is not so pleasing.

Moderation in all things.
As we all know
Eating will help you grow.
Matter evolves from condition to condition
It acquires mass and it takes up space.
It gives you an edge in the evolutionary race—
A theory-quite popular -among the herd

Although we know that we were created by God.
Many would disagree, but we do not care.
We think what we want, and we leam to share.

So, eat up now. Enjoy your crackers and dip.
When you get on the plane, there will be dinner to eat.
Which will add to your hips.

# HOMEWARD BOUND

I was on a flight home to Virginia after spending two weeks in the hospital. Suddenly we were airborne—climbing towards the cruising altitude of 37,000 feet above the grovind. I was hungry, and happy this was a dinner flight. I recognized all the commotion associated with a First Class dinner flight

Dinner at eight, dinner at eight
Do not be late.
We are serving pheasant and wine
Do not be late to dine.

The dinner bell rang, loud and clear
Summoning all those who were near
The stews all sang as the dinner bell rang
Clang, clang, clang

We are serving filet mignon and salmon too
Cooked all the way through
So as not to give you bacterium
In the 'tum'

Before we eat, we are presenting a treat
A cocktail, the old fashioned kind
Served with a twist of lemon or lime
Sublime

A martini or two may be your preferred brew
We know how to fix it
Just so
With an olive, don't you know.

If a teetotaler you are not
We will give you a shot
Of whiskey straight up, or on ice
How nice!

When dinner comes round
Turbulence causes us to bounce up and down
While wielding a carving knife
Do not fear for your life

The gent in 8A is drinking away
Singing at the top of his lungs
"No more drinking tonight. Care for Coffee?
Black or white?"

We do not care to hear more
Of that magnificent score
Much less an encore
Please do not snore.

Close your eyes, go to sleep
Forget your woes, do not weep
Night will quickly pass away
When we land it will be day

At last after a sumptuous feast
The cabin becomes dark—
The end of a lark—
      Eyes that are weary
      Eyes that are teary
      Eyes that are cheery

Slowly, slowly the lids close down
Nary a frown
They drift off into Never-Never land
Just as we planned.

# INSANITY APPROACHED

I had fainted, but everyone thought I was asleep, if they noticed or thought of me at all.

> Black, black
> The world is black
> I feel cccchills up and down my spine
> I feel cccchills up and down my back
> I think my brains are in a sack.

"Hiss hiss" went the Cat.

"I wish I were not so fat."

Just then, a weird voice appeared in my brains.

> Whrr! Whrr!
> Grrr! Grrr!
> "you may if you please, call me Sir
> I am from a planet far, far. I know you cannot get away.

> We like R and R—to get off of our craft
> We get tired of pacing fore and aft.
> The green hills of Earth, they call
> From our transporter we fall
> Until we land upon our feet.
> Transporting caimot be beat.

"Oh, my goodness, this voice is real. It is talking in English, though." I was used to talking cats and dogs, and weird phone noises, but a voice speaking English spooked me. "I had better get into the 'blueroom' so I can talk to him." I went inside, locked the door, sat down on the toilet seat, and started to communicate:

    "Who are you?"

    "I am Lufti from Mufti."

    "How can I help you?"

    Lufti replied.

    "We need to cut your brains into bits

    It takes a long, long time to do

    It takes hours before we are through."

I whipped out a cigarette, a habit when confronted with a problem. I took a puff and blew the smoke into the air. It crept under the door, into the cabin...

    Then ....

        Up, up, up it drifted

        Surrounding a passenger's coffee cup.

Bang, Bang on the door

"Why are they doing that for?"

Bang, Bang some more on the door.

"You know you cannot smoke in there,

It could cause a fire, or pollute the air."

"Okay, okay, I will put it out!

You do not need to scream and shout!"

I returned my attention to Lufti.

    "Now, Lufti, tell me more

    About what you have in store

    For little old me

    Or am I two or even three?

    I never know whether

        I am" I" or whether I am "she."

    Lufti went "whrrr."

    "I never know whether

        I am "her" or whether I am "me."

He said,

> "Your brain is slightly disarranged
> It is moderately strange
> It is moderately deranged
>
> You have lost the ability to think
> Coherently
> I do not say this
> Disparangingly
> I think you need a pill, or two, or three
> I think you need them, I really do
> At the least, you need two."

"Lufti, I certainly hope you can help me. I seem to be disassembling and no one seems to know how to help me."

"We will try. Just hang in there. Kid."

Then...

The door opened and there was a little old man
I almost forgot my plan, I almost ran
I would like to get well which would be swell!
This is too scary!
BUT
If I want to fly and not to die
I have to stay, not run away,

I was in

Ziggy's Room...

It was a dreary, dreary day
In the merry, merry month of May
My mind had been very, very far away.

I was sick and cold
Not too terribly, terribly old
Into the hospital I did go
What would happen I did not know.

I spent two weeks in the psychiatric ward
I had been sent there by the Lord.
Doctor Sung was my 'doc'
Schizophrenia gave me quite a shock.

When I got out he recommended
I
Seek psychotherapy.

So one fine day in June of 1974
I dragged myself through Ziggy's door
I was skinny and my hair was a mess
I was dressed in a pantsuit, not a dress.
I had made it myself
It was blue
I was too.

Ziggy was sitting there
Quiet and peacefiil in his leather chair.
He had white and wild hair
Me, he did not scare.

I knew he needed to hear the truth
I was living proof of
The deadly effects of
Sickness of the mind.
Ziggy and Dr. Sung were kind....

"Miss Goin, so nice to meet you. I am Dr. Lieberman. Please step into my office....why are you here?" he enquired, looking deeply into my eyes....

I babbled, unable to stop....
The Electric Zone, the Electric Zone
Of broken memories
Appears often as it pleases
It teases and teases
Leaving one to wonder and ponder.

Pondering on and on
About such existential stuff
As 'when is when' and
'enough is enough.'

That kind of stuff can be tough
To contemplate until it is late
At night when the moon
Goes cruising—providing light.

Late at night considering the why and wherefores
Of a life filled with strife
Considering the short life of a duck
Who is shot, out of luck!
His life comes to a quick end
As into the cosmos he does blend.

The voices, the voices
Where have they gone, the voices?

Here we are, in the Electric Zone
Please be nice and give this girl a bone
I'o chew and bite and spit

So as not to have a fit
The Electric Zone is new to me
But in actuality it has existed
Throughout history
Probably throughout eternity

**The End**

Printed in the United States
by Baker & Taylor Publisher Services